A BUSINESS APPROACH TO BROCCOLI FARMING

Complete Entrepreneurial Step By Step Guide To Broccoli Garden From Scratch

ZHURI HART

DISCLAIMER

This book is intended to provide general information and insights on adopting a business approach to farming. The content within is based on the author's knowledge and experiences up to the date of publication. It is essential to recognize that the field of agriculture is dynamic, influenced by various factors such as market conditions, climate, and regulatory changes.

Readers are advised to conduct thorough research, seek professional advice, and consider their unique circumstances before implementing any strategies or practices discussed in this book. The author and publisher disclaim any responsibility for the accuracy, completeness, or suitability of the information provided. The book is not a substitute for professional advice, and the author and publisher shall not be liable for any damages or losses arising from the use or reliance on the information presented herein.

Individual results may vary, and success in farming enterprises is contingent upon numerous variables. The author encourages readers to consult with relevant experts, agricultural extension services, and legal or financial professionals to tailor strategies to their specific needs and local conditions.

This book is not intended to be a comprehensive guide to all aspects of farming, and readers should exercise their judgment and discretion in applying the principles discussed. The author and publisher do not endorse any specific products, services, or companies mentioned in this book unless explicitly stated.

By reading this book, the reader acknowledges and accepts the inherent uncertainties in agricultural endeavors and agrees to use the information at their own risk.

TABLE OF CONTENTS

ABOUT THE BOOK

The book "A Business Approach to Broccoli Farming" is an all-inclusive manual for anyone wishing to work in agriculture by growing broccoli. The relevance of broccoli growing is emphasized in the book's introduction, which also discusses the crop's importance and its place in the agricultural sector. The book seeks to give readers the skills and information required to start and run a profitable broccoli farming enterprise by offering a business-oriented viewpoint.

The foundation is laid, which explains the fundamentals of broccoli growing, including the climatic and soil needs, as well as the different kinds and their traits. To make well-informed decisions regarding their growing operations, prospective broccoli farmers must possess this fundamental knowledge.

Beyond farming, of the book dives into market study, examining existing broccoli market trends, determining target consumers, and performing a competition analysis. For farmers to strategically position their broccoli fields and take advantage of current market prospects, they need to have this insight.

The book covers the practical parts of organizing and running a broccoli farm. Readers are guided through goal-setting, the creation of a thorough business plan, and the implementation of budgeting and financial planning. The growing of broccoli is the subject, which emphasizes crop rotation techniques, sustainable and organic practices, and efficient pest and disease control.

The topics of cultivation, harvesting, and quality control are shifted. Best techniques for sowing broccoli seeds, watering, fertilizing, harvesting, adhering to quality standards, evaluating, sorting, packing, and storing broccoli are given to readers.

Focus on financial management, sales and marketing, and growing the broccoli company. The book offers advice on scaling operations, diversification prospects, and partner collaboration in addition to emphasizing the creation of a brand, efficient marketing tactics, financial record-keeping, and evaluation.

Foresees obstacles in the farming of broccoli and provides solutions. The book equips readers to overcome obstacles and adjust to market swings by discussing typical problems and offering answers. To sum up, "A Business Approach to Broccoli Farming" is an invaluable tool for anyone hoping to succeed in the broccoli farming sector since it blends real-world knowledge with strategic business viewpoints.

CHAPTER ONE

BROCCOLI FARMING INTRODUCTION

THE VALUE OF BROCCOLI PRODUCTION IN THE FARMING INDUSTRY

In the agricultural sector, broccoli cultivation is important since it contributes to the world's food supply and embodies sustainable farming practices. Broccoli is a staple of the cruciferous vegetable family and is prized for its nutritional content as well as its adaptability to a wide range of culinary uses. Examining broccoli farming's benefits to the economy, nutrition, and environment is necessary to comprehend its significance.

The agricultural industry is essential to maintaining human life, and broccoli growing stands out as a major participant in this ecosystem. As a vegetable high in nutrients, broccoli offers vital vitamins, minerals, and dietary fiber. Its cultivation is essential for improving general health and correcting dietary deficits.

In addition, the market for broccoli has been rising rapidly due to customers' increased awareness of the need for wholesome, sustainable foods that are also health-conscious.

In addition to its nutritious value, broccoli production demonstrates a dedication to ecologically responsible methods. Many contemporary broccoli farms use environmentally friendly and sustainable practices, placing a strong emphasis on organic farming practices, minimal pesticide use, and effective water management. This lessens the environmental impact of conventional farming methods while simultaneously guaranteeing the creation of healthier food.

AN OUTLINE OF THE BUSINESS STRATEGY

An outline of the business strategy used in broccoli growing provides insight into the tactics farmers and other industry participants use. A thorough grasp of growing methods, consumer preferences, and market dynamics is necessary for broccoli farming to be successful. Market research is a common practice for farmers and entrepreneurs to determine trends, evaluate demand, and adjust supply.

The commercial method of growing broccoli places a premium on crop rotation, healthy soil, and effective pest control. Crop rotation improves overall yield, lowers the risk of disease, and preserves soil fertility. Adopting organic farming techniques also promotes a robust and sustainable agricultural ecosystem in addition to satisfying the growing demand for organic produce.

Market forces have a significant impact on broccoli farming's business strategy. For a broccoli-growing firm to succeed, it is vital to comprehend pricing methods, distribution routes, and consumer preferences.

To make sure their produce reaches a large audience, producers can work with supermarkets and grocery chains, attend farmers' markets, or investigate direct-to-consumer strategies.

Broccoli is more than just a healthy vegetable when it comes to the agriculture industry. It includes an all-encompassing approach to environmentally conscious company operations, sustainable farming methods, and customer-focused business strategies. The dynamic aspect of the contemporary food industry is reflected in the interplay between agriculture, nutrition, and business which is demonstrated by the growing broccoli sector.

CHAPTER TWO

KNOWING ABOUT BROCCOLI

THE FUNDAMENTALS OF AGRICULTURE AND BOTANY

Scientifically speaking, broccoli is called Brassica oleracea var. Italica is a member of the cruciferous family, which also contains Brussels sprouts, cauliflower, and cabbage. The closely packed clusters of edible flower buds, called florets, typify this green vegetable. Broccoli is classified as an annual plant in botany, having large, dark green leaves and an upright, stout stem. It goes through a special developmental phase where the edible head forms in the center of the plant and is made up of immature flower buds.

Several agricultural considerations, including soil type, temperature, and water availability, must be carefully taken into account when growing broccoli. As a cool-season crop, broccoli grows best in areas with moderate temperatures and a temperate climate.

Comprehending the life cycle of plants is essential for effective farming since farmers must plan for the best times to plant and harvest to achieve maximum productivity and quality.

DIFFERENT TYPES OF BROCCOLI AND THEIR QUALITIES

Many different types of broccoli have unique qualities to suit varying tastes and growth environments. Calabrese, Romanesco, and Purple Sprouting broccoli are common varieties. The most commonly grown variety, calabrese, has a compact, dark green head and a moderate flavor. Conversely, Romanesco is distinguished by its distinct fractal-like appearance and slightly nuttier flavor. As the name implies, purple sprouting broccoli develops green or purple florets and is generally more resilient, withstanding lower temperatures.

The intended taste and look, as well as the local soil conditions and climate, all influence the variety choice. When choosing a broccoli variety to cultivate, both farmers and gardeners take these characteristics into account to make sure it fits with the current environmental conditions and consumer demand.

CLIMATE AND BROCCOLI SOIL REQUIREMENTS

Soil quality and climate have a big impact on growing broccoli. This is a cool-season crop that can be planted in the spring or fall because it grows best around 45°F to 75°F (7°C to 24°C).

Bolting, a condition when a plant produces flowers early and reduces the quality of the harvested heads, can be brought on by excessive heat. For growth to occur at its best, there must be enough sunlight, usually at least six hours a day in direct sunlight.

Broccoli likes soil that is well-drained, rich, and has a pH range of 6.0 to 7.0, which is slightly acidic to neutral. Rich organic materials in the soil will encourage strong plant growth. Furthermore, it's critical to regulate soil moisture properly.

While continually damp soil is excellent, water logging should be avoided to avoid problems with the roots.

Successful broccoli growing requires an understanding of the complex link between broccoli and its environmental requirements. To ensure a plentiful crop of superior broccoli, farmers and gardeners must modify their techniques to fit the unique climate and soil needs.

CHAPTER THREE

EXAMINATION OF THE MARKET

CURRENT MARKET TRENDS FOR BROCCOLI

Making well-informed decisions in the field of market analysis requires a thorough grasp of the current trends in the broccoli industry. Demand for broccoli has surged recently due to a discernible shift in consumer preferences toward healthier food options. This change can be ascribed to increased knowledge of the health advantages of eating broccoli, including its high nutritional content, antioxidant capabilities, and possible anti-cancer effects. In addition, the market for broccoli has experienced a surge in demand as a result of consumers' growing inclination towards plant-based diets, which reflects shifting lifestyle preferences.

FINDING NICHE MARKETS AND TARGET AUDIENCES

A crucial component of market analysis is identifying target consumers and niche markets, especially in the context of the broccoli sector. Creating successful marketing strategies requires an understanding of the consumer base's psychographics and demographics. Health-conscious people, fitness enthusiasts, and people looking for a balanced diet are drawn to broccoli. Furthermore, finding niche markets that value organic and locally sourced goods can be a profitable tactic as demand for these qualities rises. Broccoli farmers can create a more targeted and significant market presence by focusing their marketing efforts on these segments.

AN EXAMINATION OF COMPETITION IN THE BROCCOLI FARMING SECTOR

An essential tool for assessing a company's potential advantages, disadvantages, opportunities, and threats in the broccoli growing sector is competitive analysis. Key players, their market share, and their strategy are revealed by analyzing the landscape. The competitive dynamics are influenced by several variables, including price strategies, production techniques, and geographic distribution. Gaining a competitive edge also requires remaining aware of technological developments in farming methods and distribution systems. The broccoli farming sector is a dynamic one, and profitability and sustainability depend heavily on innovation and efficiency. Industry participants can enhance their strategies, set themselves apart from the competition, and position themselves strategically for success in this dynamic market by acknowledging the competitive environment.

Market analysis in the broccoli industry entails a careful examination of the most recent developments, consumer profiles, and competition landscape. By exploring these aspects, interested parties can come up with smart plans to take advantage of the growing demand for healthier eating options, reach specialized markets, and move quickly and strategically through the competitive landscape.

CHAPTER FOUR

ORGANIZING YOUR FARM TO GROW BROCCOLI

ESTABLISHING OBJECTIVES AND GOALS

An essential first step in organizing your broccoli farm is to set attainable goals. Start by outlining the general goals of your farm and the things you hope to accomplish in the near and distant future. Take into account elements like the target market, production volume, and sustainability policies.

Objectives can be raising the yield of broccoli, reaching a wider market, or using environmentally friendly farming practices. Setting SMART (specific, measurable, achievable, relevant, and time-bound) goals will help you stay on course with your agricultural pursuits.

MAKING AN ALL-INCLUSIVE BUSINESS PLAN:

The framework for your broccoli farm is a well-considered business plan, which will guide you through the challenges of agricultural entrepreneurship. Begin by describing the goals and objectives of your farm, including the goods and services you plan to provide. To find competitors, assess potential obstacles, and determine the demand for broccoli, do a full market analysis. Establish your target market and create a marketing plan that complements the special features of your farm.

Provide an organizational structure in your company strategy that describes important staff roles and duties as well as any partnerships or collaborations. Talk about the operational elements as well, including where your farm is located, how big the area is, and what tools or technology are required for productive farming.

Describe the entire production process, including the selection of seeds, harvesting, and distribution. Incorporating a thorough risk management strategy that takes into account variables like the weather, pests, and market swings is also important.

FINANCIAL PLANNING AND BUDGETING

Financial planning and budgeting are essential components of running a profitable broccoli farm. Create a thorough budget that takes into consideration all projected costs, such as labor, equipment, land acquisition, seeds, fertilizer, and marketing. Make sure your financial projection is reasonable by accounting for any unforeseen expenses.

Review and revise your budget regularly to account for unforeseen events, changes in the market, and manufacturing costs.

Examine government programs that promote agricultural efforts and think about obtaining financial support through grants or loans.

Create a method to monitor income and expenses, using accounting software if required. Use effective money management techniques to make sure your farm business can survive.

Examine your broccoli farm's financial statements regularly to assess its performance and make well-informed decisions for future expansion and profitability.

CHAPTER FIVE

METHODS OF FARMING BROCCOLI

ORGANIC AND SUSTAINABLE FARMING METHODS

Organic and sustainable farming methods that emphasize environmental health and reduce the use of artificial inputs can greatly boost broccoli production. Techniques used in sustainable agriculture support biodiversity, preserve water, and preserve soil fertility. Particularly, organic farming does not employ artificial fertilizers or pesticides; instead, it depends entirely on natural processes.

Soil management is an essential component of sustainable broccoli production. Farmers improve the fertility and structure of their soil by using practices like cover crops and the incorporation of organic materials. In addition to adding organic matter and preventing soil erosion, cover crops also reduce weeds and provide a healthy, nutrient-rich growing environment for broccoli plants.

Natural fertilizers, such as compost and manure, are vital to the organic broccoli farming process since they supply the soil with vital nutrients. Additionally, crop leftovers are recycled to improve soil structure and hold onto moisture. These methods help to lessen their negative effects on the environment while also maintaining the health of the soil.

CROP ROTATION TECHNIQUES

To protect soil health and lessen the effects of pests and diseases, crop rotation is a crucial technique in the production of broccoli. Crop rotation is the process of gradually switching up the kinds of crops cultivated in a particular location. By disrupting their reproductive cycles and lowering the amount of pathogens that accumulate in the soil, this tactic aids in breaking the cycles of disease and pests.

A well-thought-out crop rotation plan for broccoli farming might alternate broccoli with diverse plant groups. For example, planting broccoli in rotation with legumes like beans or peas will help fix nitrogen in the soil, which will benefit broccoli crops in the future. Furthermore, adding cover crops to the rotation cycle improves the structure and fertility of the soil.

To limit the depletion of particular nutrients in the soil, effective crop rotation methods also take into account the nutritional requirements of various crops. By lowering the danger of soil-borne illnesses and decreasing the need for synthetic fertilizers, this all-encompassing strategy supports sustainable agriculture.

MANAGEMENT OF PESTS AND DISEASES

Controlling illnesses and pests is essential to productive broccoli farming. Finding a balance between pest control and environmental sustainability can be facilitated by implementing integrated pest management (IPM) techniques. To reduce the impact of pests while limiting harm to beneficial creatures and the environment, integrated pest management (IPM) integrates biological, cultural, and chemical control strategies.

Utilizing diseases, parasites, or natural predators to manage pest populations is known as biological control. For instance, introducing predatory mites or ladybugs can help manage aphid infestations in broccoli crops. Cultural control techniques include planting at the appropriate distance from one another, rotating crops, and choosing broccoli cultivars that are resistant to disease.

Although it is a part of integrated pest management, chemical treatment is used sparingly in sustainable broccoli cultivation. When using pesticides, farmers choose organic options and adhere to specified application rates to reduce their influence on the environment. For prompt response and efficient management, crops must be routinely inspected for early indications of pests or diseases.

CHAPTER SIX

GROWING AND GATHERING

PLANTING SEEDS AND SEEDLINGS OF BROCCOLI:

When planting broccoli, timing, soil, and propagation strategy must all be carefully considered. It is possible to produce broccoli from seeds or seedlings, and each has advantages of its own. It is essential to start seeds indoors 6–8 weeks before the last anticipated frost date in the area when planting seeds. Plant broccoli seeds in pots or trays using a seed-starting mixture that drains well. For germination, the seeds need constant moisture and temperature, usually about 70°F (21°C).

When broccoli seedlings are between four and six inches tall and have at least two true leaves, they are ready to be transplanted into the outdoor garden. Since broccoli is a cool-season crop, planting should be planned to expose the seedlings to milder temperatures. It is advised that plants be spaced 18 to 24 inches apart to allow for proper air circulation and to prevent infections.

METHODS OF FERTILIZATION AND IRRIGATION

Water and nutrients are two things that broccoli plants specifically need to grow and yield high-quality heads. Since broccoli has shallow roots and might become stressed by a lack of water, it is important to provide it with enough water, especially during dry times. For optimal head development, there should be a consistent supply of moisture; one inch of water per week is typically advised. It is best to use soaker hoses or drip irrigation rather than drenching the leaves, as this can result in fungal diseases.

Broccoli cultivation is largely dependent on effective fertilization techniques. To ensure adequate drainage and nutrient availability, it is recommended to treat the soil with organic matter before planting. A balanced fertilizer application is best for broccoli, usually with higher nitrogen content.

During the growing season, fertilizer applied as a side dressing can help the plant meet its nutritional requirements. Regular soil monitoring is essential, and fertilization techniques should be modified in response to plant growth and health.

THE BEST METHODS FOR BROCCOLI HARVESTING

Timely harvesting of broccoli is essential to preserving its optimal flavor and freshness in the heads. The broccoli variety and the surrounding conditions determine when to harvest.

Broccoli heads are usually ready to be harvested when they are compact and the buds are still tightly closed. Postponing the harvest could lead to loose, open floret formation and an unpleasant flavor.

When harvesting broccoli, cut the main head at an angle with a sharp knife or shears, leaving a few inches of stalk attached. This makes it possible for smaller, secondary heads to form. Harvesting the main head before the individual flowers open is imperative. Harvesting on a regular and timely basis encourages continued output, and as side shoots grow, more harvest opportunities may arise. To preserve freshness and flavor, store broccoli in the refrigerator after harvesting.

CHAPTER SEVEN

ASSURANCE AND QUALITY CONTROL

PUTTING QUALITY STANDARDS INTO PRACTICE

Putting quality standards into practice is essential to guaranteeing the regular provision of high-caliber goods or services. A product or service's acceptable performance, features, and qualities are defined by quality standards, which operate as benchmarks. Implementing quality standards necessitates developing a methodical strategy for process monitoring, assessment, and improvement. This could entail creating and recording best practices, rules, and standardized processes that adhere to the established quality standards.

All stakeholders in an organization must be committed to and involved in the implementation of quality standards for it to be effective. This covers the administration, staff, vendors, and clients. To make sure that everyone is aware of the significance of upholding quality standards and their part in preserving the general level of product or service quality, communication and training initiatives are frequently necessary. To track compliance and pinpoint areas in need of ongoing improvement, audits, and assessments are carried out regularly.

EXAMINING AND CLASSIFYING BROCCOLI

Broccoli inspection and grading is an essential part of the food industry's quality control procedure. Broccoli must be thoroughly inspected to determine its size, color, texture, and general look. This procedure aids in locating any flaws, anomalies, or departures from defined standards of quality. Inspections can happen at many points along the supply chain, from the farm to the distribution and processing hubs.

Broccoli is graded according to predefined standards of quality. Through this classification, consumers are guaranteed access to only those products that fulfill particular quality standards.

The grading procedure may consider elements such as freshness, size, color consistency, and defect-free status. Having a strong inspection and grading system in place ensures that only broccoli of the highest caliber is sold, which increases customer satisfaction.

ASPECTS TO TAKE INTO ACCOUNT FOR PACKAGING AND STORAGE

Throughout a product's lifecycle, proper packaging and storage are essential components in preserving its quality. In addition to shielding the goods from environmental elements like moisture, contamination, and physical harm, proper packaging makes sure the product reaches customers in the best possible shape. The product's specifications as well as industry norms should be taken into consideration while selecting the packaging materials and techniques.

The goal of storage considerations is to maintain the product's quality and shelf life by generating ideal circumstances. Storage conditions are mostly determined by variables including temperature, humidity, and ventilation. In storage facilities, putting quality control procedures in place helps stop deterioration, spoiling, and other types of damage. Furthermore, inventory management systems help ensure that products are rotated efficiently, reducing the possibility that damaged or expired goods will reach final customers.

A thorough quality control and assurance system must include the effective application of quality standards, thorough broccoli inspection and grading procedures, and careful packing and storage considerations. When combined, these strategies help produce goods that either match or surpass consumer expectations, fostering brand loyalty and guaranteeing sustained market success.

CHAPTER EIGHT

SALES AND MARKETING

CREATING A BRAND FOR YOUR FARM OF BROCCOLI

Creating a unique brand for your broccoli farm is essential in the cutthroat agriculture industry of today. A brand is more than simply a name or logo; it includes your company's identity, values, and reputation. The first step in building a strong brand for your broccoli farm is figuring out what makes it special.

Emphasize the qualities that make your produce stand out, such as sustainable cultivation techniques, excellent quality, or organic agricultural practices. Create an engaging brand narrative that highlights the farm's dedication to community, sustainability, and wellness.

Think about making a professional branding investment, such as a distinctive logo, eye-catching packaging, and messaging that is consistent throughout all media. Customers should be able to connect with your brand and feel good about it, which will increase the likelihood that they will select your broccoli over other brands.

To humanize your brand, interact with your target population through social media, content marketing, and neighborhood gatherings. Showcase the behind-the-scenes parts of your farm.

SUCCESSFUL MARKETING TECHNIQUES

Driving sales and advertising your broccoli farm requires a well-thought-out marketing plan. To begin with, gather information about customer trends, preferences, and the competitive environment by performing market research. Determine who your target market is and then focus your marketing efforts on appealing to their wants and needs. To reach a large audience, make use of a variety of outlets, including grocery shops, farmers' markets, and internet platforms.

In today's corporate environment, digital marketing is crucial. Create a user-friendly website about your broccoli farm that includes eye-catching graphics and educational content.

Use social media to interact with your target market, provide updates about your produce, and launch focused marketing efforts. Think about working with dietitians or influencers who can vouch for the health advantages of broccoli and help you reach a larger audience with your brand.

Tell a compelling story those appeals to your target audience by incorporating storytelling into your marketing plan. Talk about your experiences, testimonials, and the transformation of your broccoli from the field to the table. Draw attention to the health advantages and countless culinary uses for broccoli. Providing special offers, rebates, or loyalty plans can further encourage customers to regularly select your vegetables.

DEVELOPING CONNECTIONS WITH DISTRIBUTORS AND PURCHASERS:

Building trusting relationships with distributors and purchasers is critical to your broccoli farm's long-term success. Find possible partners who share your beliefs and are in your target market to start. Make connections with distributors and buyers by going to trade exhibits, industry events, and networking gatherings. Make sure to express to your customers the benefits that your broccoli offers and your farm's unique selling characteristics.

Develop a trustworthy and uniform supply chain by offering distributors and customers' dependable solutions. Make sure your broccoli satisfies quality requirements, and communicate openly about your agricultural methods. Relationships can be strengthened by providing samples, giving farm tours, or taking part in joint marketing campaigns.

Being adaptable is essential when interacting with distributors and buyers. Adjust to their shifting requirements, inclinations, and market conditions. Stay receptive to criticism and always look for methods to make your goods and services better. Developing a reputation for dependability, excellence, and teamwork will establish your broccoli farm as a go-to source, resulting in enduring collaborations and steady market expansion.

CHAPTER NINE

ACCOUNTING AND RECORD-KEEPING

PROCEDURES IN FINANCIAL MANAGEMENT

Effective financial management requires the use of record-keeping and accounting practices, which offer a methodical way to organize and record financial transactions in a business, such as a broccoli farm.

A business owner can monitor revenue, expenses, and overall financial success by keeping precise records. Every financial activity, including purchases, sales, and expenses, must be consistently and methodically recorded during this process.

Adopting good record-keeping procedures makes decision-making easier by giving a clear picture of the financial situation. In addition to supporting daily operations, timely and accurate financial records are essential for financial analysis, tax filings, and audits. This process can be streamlined by using accounting software or by engaging qualified accountants, assuring adherence to legal requirements, and promoting openness within the context of financial management.

ASSESSING THE STABILITY OF YOUR BROCCOLI FARM'S CASH

Analyzing a variety of financial measures is necessary to evaluate the entire performance and sustainability of a broccoli farm to determine its financial health. Key performance metrics including income, costs, profit margins, and return on investment provide light on how profitable the farm is. Furthermore, assessing the farm's liquidity, solvency, and efficiency ratios aids in determining its capacity to pay short-term loans, manage resources effectively, and meet other commitments.

Risk management and market movements are included in the assessment of financial health, which goes beyond numerical analysis. Strategic planning and risk avoidance are made possible by an understanding of the external elements, such as weather, consumer demand, and regulatory changes that may have an impact on the broccoli market. Frequent assessments of financial health enable farmers to make well-informed decisions, adjust to changing market conditions, and strengthen the business's overall resilience.

GETTING FINANCES AND MANAGING THEM

A broccoli farm's ability to survive and grow depends on its ability to secure funding and manage its finances. To show the farm's viability and possible return on investment, a thorough financial strategy is necessary when applying for loans, luring investors, or investigating government handouts. Funding requests gain credibility when a thorough business plan including financial estimates, market analysis, and risk management techniques is developed.

Strategic financial planning, cash flow management, and budgeting are all included in financial management. A realistic budget makes it easier to prioritize investments, manage spending, and distribute resources effectively. Sufficient cash flow management guarantees the availability of funding for investments as well as daily operations. Long-term financial goals, expansion prospects, and market situation adaptation are all part of strategic financial planning.

A broccoli farm's financial management structure should incorporate strong accounting and record-keeping procedures, ongoing assessments of the farm's financial health, and tactical methods for raising capital and handling cash flow. Farm owners can successfully negotiate the complexity of the agricultural industry, make wise judgments, and promote sustainable growth by putting these ideas into practice.

CHAPTER TEN

GROWING YOUR BROCCOLI ENTERPRISE

GROWING YOUR FARMING BUSINESS

To satisfy rising demand and seize market opportunities, you must strategically expand your farming operations to scale your broccoli business. Growing the amount of land used for broccoli farming is a crucial component of this expansion. To guarantee ideal growing circumstances, carefully evaluate the soil quality, climate, and water availability in prospective new locations. Using contemporary farming methods and technologies, such as controlled-environment farming and precision agriculture, can also increase output and efficiency.

Purchasing infrastructure is essential for growing your farming business. This entails modernizing irrigation systems, constructing more storage spaces, and purchasing cutting-edge machinery for broccoli cultivation, harvesting, and processing. Hiring more experienced workers can be necessary when you scale up to handle the extra workload and keep your broccoli produce up to par.

Create a thorough plan that takes into account both short- and long-term objectives, accounting for things like market trends and seasonal variances.

OPPORTUNITIES FOR DIVERSIFICATION

Investigating new revenue sources and product lines is part of diversifying your broccoli business. Think about adding value-added broccoli goods to your lineup, like frozen broccoli, packed and pre-cut broccoli florets, or broccoli-based snacks.

To find creative ways to introduce broccoli to a larger audience, investigate specialty markets and consumer preferences. Furthermore, diversification can entail experimenting with different crops that go well with broccoli or breaking into allied agricultural pursuits like organic farming or agro tourism.

industry research is necessary to detect gaps in the industry, evaluate competition, and comprehend consumer expectations to effectively diversify. Talk to your current clientele to get their opinions on possible new offerings. Work together with food scientists and culinary specialists to create distinctive and enticing broccoli-based products that satisfy changing customer preferences. Diversification helps to position your broccoli firm as a flexible and adaptable competitor in the agriculture industry while also reducing the risks connected with market volatility.

COOPERATION & JOINT VENTURES

Establishing alliances and working together are crucial to growing your broccoli business. Creating partnerships with other farmers, farming associations, and academic institutions can give access to pooled resources, information, and experience. Working together can result in pooled distribution networks, cooperative marketing techniques, and cooperative input purchases, all of which can lower costs and boost productivity. To get good terms for large purchases, think about joining agricultural cooperatives or partnering with suppliers.

Forming alliances with distributors and retailers is essential to reaching a wider audience. To guarantee a consistent and extensive distribution of your broccoli goods, collaborate closely with supermarket chains, eateries, and food service providers. Work together with chefs and food influencers to highlight the nutritional value and adaptability of broccoli, building a favorable reputation and raising consumer awareness. Furthermore, investigate cooperative research initiatives to remain current with technology developments and environmentally friendly agricultural methods.

Growing your broccoli business needs a diversified strategy that includes growing your farming operations, looking at prospects for diversification, and encouraging cooperation and partnerships within the agricultural ecosystem.

CHAPTER ELEVEN

PROBLEMS AND SOLUTIONS

TYPICAL OBSTACLES IN BROCCOLI FARMING

Like any agricultural venture, broccoli cultivation has several obstacles that could affect its profitability and productivity. Among the main difficulties is the presence of pests.

Aphids, caterpillars, and flea beetles are just a few of the pests that can harm broccoli plants and lower yields. For broccoli farmers, managing pests in a sustainable and environmentally friendly way is an ongoing problem.

Unfavorable weather is another frequent problem. Broccoli grows best in cool climates; it can be adversely affected by intense heat or cold. Unpredictable weather patterns, like sudden frosts or extended hot spells, might interfere with broccoli crops' regular growth, resulting in lower quality and fewer harvests.

Broccoli growing depends heavily on the quality of the soil, and keeping the ideal soil conditions can be difficult. Problems like nutrient deficiency, soil erosion, and soil-borne illnesses can affect broccoli plants' ability to develop and stay healthy. Farmers must adopt efficient soil management techniques to tackle these issues and guarantee the enduring viability of their crops.

TECHNIQUES FOR SOLVING PROBLEMS

Farmers use a range of problem-solving techniques to increase crop resilience and boost total production to overcome the obstacles associated with growing broccoli. To effectively manage pests, integrated pest management (IPM) is a comprehensive technique that combines chemical, biological, and cultural control strategies. Farmers can reduce the impact of pests on broccoli harvests while increasing environmental sustainability by using natural predators, crop rotation, and properly chosen herbicides.

Another tactic to reduce the risk brought on by unfavorable weather is crop diversity. Broccoli comes in a variety of temperature- and climate-tolerant types that farmers can plant, offering some protection from adverse weather. Furthermore, farmers can take preventative action when unfavorable weather conditions are predicted by investing in early warning systems and weather monitoring technology.

Farmers use organic amendments and cover crops, among other sustainable farming techniques, to solve problems with soil health. Cover crops contribute to improved nutrient retention, reduced soil erosion, and improved soil structure overall. Farmers can restore nutrients to the soil and foster a healthy growth environment for broccoli by adding organic matter to the soil through composting and other techniques.

GETTING PAST MARKET VOLATILITY

Market swings affect the price and demand for broccoli production, which is a major concern for growers.

Farmers can use supply chain management and creative marketing to combat these swings. Broccoli products can have a more stable market if distributors, merchants, and local marketplaces are well-connected.

It is essential to diversify market channels to lessen reliance on any one market and to lessen the impact of price volatility. Examining alternatives like direct-to-consumer sales, farmers' markets, and community-supported agriculture (CSA) can give broccoli producers another way to market their products and build a more durable brand.

To solve market difficulties, cooperation within the broccoli farming community is also essential. Growers can pool resources for marketing initiatives, share market data, and collectively negotiate better prices through the use of farmers' groups and cooperatives. Farmers may more successfully manage market swings and secure a lucrative and sustainable future for broccoli cultivation by banding together.